Rosh Hashanah and Yom Kippur

By David F. Marx

Consultants
Nanci R. Vargus, Ed.D.
Primary Multiage Teacher
Decatur Township Schools, Indianapolis, Indiana

Katharine A. Kane, Reading Specialist
Former Language Arts Coordinator,
San Diego County Office of Education

Children's Press®
A Division of Scholastic Inc.
New York   Toronto   London   Auckland   Sydney
Mexico City   New Delhi   Hong Kong
Danbury, Connecticut

Designer: Herman Adler Design
Photo Researcher: Caroline Anderson
The photo on the cover shows a young girl blowing the shofar.

Library of Congress Cataloging-in-Publication Data

Marx, David F.
    Rosh Hashanah and Yom Kippur / by David F. Marx.
      p. cm. — (Rookie read-about holidays)
    Includes index.
    ISBN 0-516-22266-X (lib. bdg.)   0-516-26313-7 (pbk.)
    1. High Holidays—Juvenile literature. [Rosh ha-Shanah. 2. Yom
Kippur. 3. Holidays. 4. Fasts and feasts—Judaism.] I. Title. II. Series.
BM693.H5 M39   2001
296.4'31—dc21
                          00-057036

CHILDREN'S PRESS, and ROOKIE READ-ABOUT®,
and associated logos are trademarks and or registered trademarks
of Scholastic Library Publishing. SCHOLASTIC and associated logos
are trademarks and or registered trademarks of Scholastic Inc.
  4 5 6 7 8 9 10 R 10 09 08 07 06 05 04

Rosh Hashanah (ROSH huh-SHAH-nuh) and Yom Kippur (YOM kee-POOR) are two holidays celebrated by people of the Jewish faith.

These two holidays are ten days apart. They always fall in September or October each year.

Together, Rosh Hashanah and Yom Kippur are called the High Holy Days.

September 2004

Sunday	Monday	Tuesday	Wednesday	Thursday	Friday	Saturday
			1	2	3	4
5	6	7	8	9	10	11
12	13	14	**15**	16	17	18
19	20	21	22	23	**24**	25
26	27	28	29	30		

Rosh Hashanah is September 15, 2004.
Yom Kippur is September 24, 2004.

Rosh Hashanah is the beginning of the Jewish new year. It is an important time.

Jewish people eat apples dipped in honey for a "sweet new year."

Jews gather at buildings called synagogues (SIN-uh-gogs) for special services led by a rabbi.

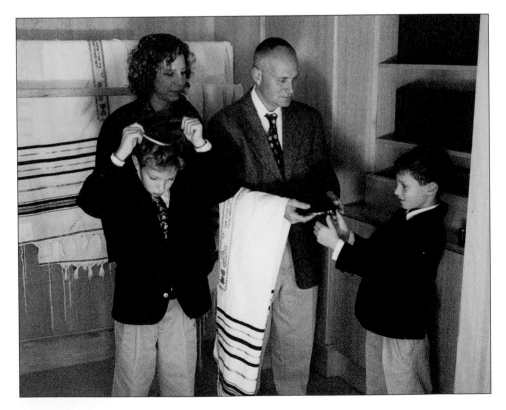

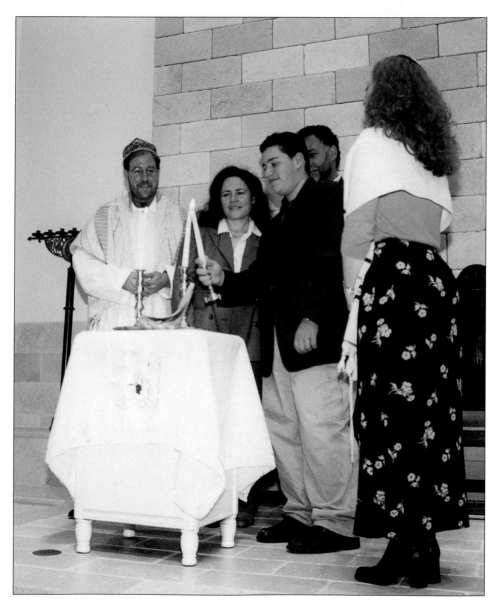

9

The rabbi blows a ram's horn to call the people together. This horn is called a shofar (SHOW-far).

The rabbi reads from the Torah (TOR-uh). The Torah tells the history of the Jewish people.

The Torah contains old stories about Moses, Abraham, Isaac, and many others.

Abraham, on the right, with Isaac

Rosh Hashanah lasts
two days.

Ten days later is the
next High Holy Day,
Yom Kippur.

The days between the
two holidays are called
the Days of Awe.

Yom Kippur is a quiet time
for thinking and praying.

Many Jews fast. That
means they do not eat
during the day.

On Yom Kippur, Jews remember relatives and friends who have died.

They also think about how they treated others during the year. Were they kind? Did they keep the promises they made?

Many people think of
good things they can
do in the new year.

In the Yom Kippur service, people sing a special song about how to be a good person.

It is the *Kol Nidre* (KOL NEE-dra).

When the sun sets at the end of Yom Kippur, the High Holy Days are over.

Then the Jews share a meal to end their fast.

On Rosh Hashanah and Yom Kippur, Jewish people think about the past year.

They decide how they might change things in the year to come.

They say, "L'Shanah Tovah!" A Happy New Year!

Words You Know

Abraham and Isaac

apples

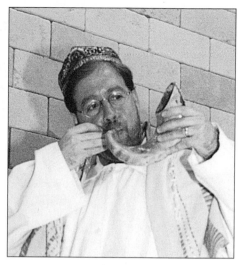

shofar

synagogue

Torah

31

Index

About the Author

David F. Marx is an author and editor of children's books.
He resides in the Chicago area.

Photo Credits

Photographs ©: Bridgeman Art Library International Ltd., London/New York: 15, 30 (EDI81506/Private Collection); Corbis-Bettmann: 24, 31 bottom left (Reuters); Dan Brody: 8, 9, 11, 31 top right; Liaison Agency, Inc.: 21 (Bob Schatz); Post Stock/The Palm Beach Post: 28 (Palm Beach Daily News); Photodisk: 27; PhotoEdit: 19 (Robert Brenner), 18 (Felicia Martinez), 22 (D. Young-Wolfe); Randy Matusow: cover, 3, 6, 16, 31 top left; Stock Boston: 23 (Spencer Grant), 12, 31 bottom right (Herb Snitzer).

Special thanks to the Brooklyn Heights Synagogue, Brooklyn, New York.